The Royal Navy

Andrew Langley

The Armed Forces

The Army
The Royal Air Force
The Royal Navy

Cover   HMS *Ark Royal*.

First published in 1986 by
Wayland (Publishers) Limited
61 Western Road, Hove,
East Sussex, BN3 1JD, England

© Copyright 1986 Wayland (Publishers) Ltd

British Library Cataloguing in Publication Data
Langley, Andrew
  The Royal Navy.——(The Armed forces)
  1. Great Britain. *Royal Navy*——Juvenile literature
  I. Title   II. Series
  359'.00941   VA454

ISBN 0-85078-883-8

Phototypeset by The Bath Press, Avon
Printed in Italy by G. Canale & C.S.p.A., Turin
Bound in the UK at The Bath Press, Avon

Contents

The Royal Navy Today	4	Warships	22
The Navy in History	6	Aircraft and Weapons	24
The Front Line	8	The Navy and the World	26
The Support Branches	10	The Future	28
The Royal Marines	12	Glossary	30
Joining the Royal Navy	14	Further Information	31
A Sailor's Day	16	Books to Read	31
On Exercise	18	Index	32
The Promotion Ladder	20		

The Royal Navy Today

Today, the Royal Navy is the third most powerful naval force in the world, after the USA and the Soviet Union. Its main task is to keep its country safe from invasion. But, in order to do this effectively, it also has to help defend Western Europe.

The United Kingdom is part of the North Atlantic Treaty Organization (NATO). This is a pact between a group of nations, which includes the USA, West Germany and Canada. They have agreed to help each other if one of them is threatened by another country. Most NATO forces are based in West Germany, on the border with Eastern Europe.

The ships and personnel of the Royal Navy are a vital part of these NATO forces. They are small in number, totalling less than seventy thousand men and women, about fifty frigates and destroyers, and

The flight-deck of the aircraft carrier HMS Illustrious.

thirty-four submarines. But the Navy is equipped with a huge variety of powerful weapons, including nuclear missiles, and every member is highly skilled in his or her branch of operations.

Nearly all the Navy's strength is committed to NATO and to the protection of the trade routes of the North Atlantic. In peacetime, it also keeps an eye on offshore oilfields and gas platforms, and safeguards British fishery rights.

The Royal Navy is known as 'the Senior Service', because it is the oldest of Britain's armed forces. It has defended the shores of this country and protected its sea routes for many centuries. In fact, without the power of the Navy, British history might have been very different.

A Lynx *helicopter with HMS* Sirius *on patrol in the North Atlantic.*

The Navy in History

Alfred the Great was the first British king to realize the importance of sea power. When faced by the threat of invasion from the Vikings, in about AD 895, he built and organized a large fleet of ships. With this, he was able to defeat the raiders before they could set foot on British shores.

For many centuries, sea battles were settled by hand-to-hand fighting. Soldiers were carried on ships to board and capture enemy vessels. However, the invention of the cannon brought about a great change. Because seamen could fire the new weapons themselves, soldiers were no longer needed. Ships grew in size, so that they could carry as many guns as possible.

The golden age of the Navy stretched over three centuries and could be said to have begun with the defeat of the Spanish Armada,

French and British warships fight at close quarters at Trafalgar in 1805.

in 1588. The country's growing naval strength helped it to establish the British Empire and to open up new trading routes. Naval bases were established in Canada, the West Indies, India and many other countries.

After defeating the French at Trafalgar, in 1805, Britain really did 'rule the waves'. Yet her sailors lived in wretched conditions. Their quarters were cramped and airless, and they were fed on stale food and foul water. Discipline was very harsh and crew members were often beaten. When a ship needed extra men, 'press gangs' were used to forced them to join up.

Working conditions improved greatly for sailors at the beginning of this century. The ships changed too – steam power replaced sail and the first 'ironclads', or armoured ships, were built. During the two World Wars (1914–18; 1939–45), the Royal Navy protected merchant shipping from enemy submarines, and made sure that Britain was supplied with food and raw materials. However, by the end of the Second World War, the era of the big battleships was ending. Air power was gradually becoming more important than sea power.

HMS Dreadnought, *built in 1906, was the most powerful battleship of its day*.

The Front Line

A modern warship needs a small, but highly-trained crew. The huge variety of weapons and equipment on board requires expert handling. The Navy's 'front-line' operations at sea are performed by the Operations Branch (made up of the Seaman and Communications Groups) and by the Fleet Air Arm.

Seaman Group
Seamen have to 'work' and 'fight' their ship. 'Working' involves all the skills of steering, navigating and looking after a vessel at sea. 'Fighting', of course, includes the firing of guns and missiles, and keeping a close watch on the enemy.

Seamen are trained to specialize in one of the following jobs:
   Diver (clearing mines and making underwater checks).
   Electronic Warfare (intercepting

enemy radio messages).
Mine Warfare (clearing mines).
Missile Warfare (controlling the ship's weapons).
Radar (observing the positions of other ships and aircraft).
Sonar (hunting for submarines).
Survey (research for Naval charts and maps).

Communications Group
It is vitally important for a ship to keep in radio contact with shore bases, with other ships and with aircraft. By using many different types of equipment, radio operators can send messages to almost any part of the world. They can also communicate with nearby ships by the use of flashing lights and loud-hailers.

Fleet Air Arm
Aircraft are becoming increasingly important to the Navy. The Fleet Air Arm flies and maintains the fighters and helicopters which take off from aircraft carriers, frigates and land bases.

The Support Branches

Both the ships and the men in the front line have to be prepared for action at all times. They therefore rely heavily on the work of the engineers, the supply and secretarial staff, and teams who form the support branches of the service.

Engineering
The Navy uses some very advanced equipment, such as nuclear-powered submarines and radar-guided missiles. Naturally, such complex machinery needs to be serviced and repaired regularly. Engineers are specially trained to deal with a ship's various systems, or with its weapons, or with the aircraft operated by the Fleet Air Arm.

Supply
The job of the Supply Branch is to make sure that each ship is run efficiently. Clerks, called 'writers', deal with the paperwork involved in preparing

accounts and wages. Store accountants keep track of the huge stock of spare items and parts that might be needed, from boots to warheads. Cooks and stewards prepare and serve meals to the crew.

Medical
Each ship carries its own medical staff, and the Royal Navy has several special hospitals on the mainland. These are staffed by doctors, dentists and a full range of technicians. There is also a special Naval nursing service.

Women's Royal Naval Service (WRNS)
Known as the 'Wrens' for short, the women of the WRNS do most of the support jobs alongside men. These include engineering (maintaining and repairing aircraft), clerical (such as accountancy, plotting Naval exercises, preparing detailed forecasts of weather and shipping conditions) and communications work (transport, telephone and radio operations). Wrens, however, do not serve in warships at sea.

The Royal Marines

The Corps of Royal Marines is almost as old as the Royal Navy itself. For over three hundred years it has been the Navy's infantry force, ready to strike swiftly on land or at sea.

The Marines provide 'commandos' of highly trained soldiers. These commandos can go into action anywhere in the world – in jungles, snow covered regions, or in crowded cities. They carry with them their own special equipment and often work alongside units of the British Army.

The Marines are at the head of any landing force. They travel from their assault ships to the shore in

Rifle practice for Marines in Norway.

Marine commandos on the Falklands.

A beach landing in lightweight boats.

Exercises on board HMS Hermes.

landing craft, or smaller boats. They are skilled in rock-climbing, skiing and swimming. For smaller, secret operations, the experts of the Special Boat Service (SBS) are used.

Becoming a Marine is no easy matter. All candidates have to go through a tough test of strength and character, which lasts for three days. Those who pass spend eight months at the Commando Training Centre in Devon. At the end of this period, they are presented with the famous green beret of the fully trained commando.

The Marines also provide the Navy with music. The Band of the Royal Marines is famous throughout the world. It appears at concerts, cup finals and state occasions, as well as on radio and television. Most bandsmen can play at least two instruments.

Joining the Royal Navy

Most people first find out about the Navy by visiting their local Royal Navy Careers Office. Here they can discuss service life and prospects with members of the staff. If they wish to join up, they then spend a day taking some routine tests at the Careers Office. These will help the staff to decide which branch of the Navy a person is best suited to. Candidates are also given a medical examination to make sure they are fit and healthy.

Not everyone will be accepted as

A recruit takes his first ride on an aerial ropeway.

a recruit. Those who fail the tests or who are thought unsuited to Naval life are turned down. The successful ones are given a certificate and are allowed to begin basic training.

A rating's first eleven weeks are spent at HMS *Raleigh*, a land base near Plymouth (a non-seaman spends seven weeks there). He is given his uniforms and is taught how to march on parade. He learns the basic skills of seafaring, such as ropework, handling a small boat and life-raft drill. Most important of all, he learns how to obey orders quickly and efficiently.

After basic training, a recruit goes on to learn his special trade. This can take anything from six weeks (for a steward) to seventeen weeks (for an engineering mechanic). Most seamen join up with their first ship after about nine months.

Women who wish to join the WRNS spend five weeks at HMS *Raleigh*. After basic training, which is similar to that given to men, they are able to transfer to one of the special branches – Operations, Supply and Secretariat, Dental, Fleet Air Arm or General Support. Although they do not serve at sea, members of the WRNS are involved in all other aspects of life in the Royal Navy.

A WRNS engineer checks the engine of a Wessex *helicopter.*

A Sailor's Day

At sea, a ship has to be operated twenty-four hours a day. The day is divided into 'watches' or shifts, so that everyone has their fair share of duty and of time off.

Depending on the type of ship – a protection or survey vessel, a destroyer or a frigate – there will be special duties for the crew to perform. There are, however,

A gun-crew practise anti-aircraft fire during a ship exercise.

tasks common to all ships. On the bridge, navigators keep the ship on the right course. In the radar room, seamen watch the positions of aircraft and other vessels in the area. Down in the engine room, engineers look after the machinery and power systems.

In addition to their normal duties, members of the crew will have to take part in many exercises. This might be firing live missiles, hunting submarines, skin-diving, practising battle operations or perhaps learning about radar or navigation.

At sea, a sailor's life is highly disciplined and his training must prepare him to cope with any situation – a battle, a rescue operation or an emergency on board ship. He must always be alert when on duty, literally 'on watch'.

Conditions on board a modern warship have improved a lot since the days of sail. Seamen now sleep in comfortable bunks instead of hammocks, and their quarters are air-conditioned. There is plenty of good food to eat, lots to do during periods off-duty, and at least five weeks holiday each year.

The operations room of the destroyer, HMS Bristol.

On Exercise

The men and women of the Royal Navy are always in training. They learn to handle their ships, aircraft and weapons as skilfully as possible so that they are ready for any emergency that might arise. To practise these skills in a war-like situation, special 'mock' battles, called exercises, are organized.

A big NATO exercise may involve over 50,000 people, 150 ships and 400 aircraft. These would be drawn from the navies of several countries. One group of ships acts as the 'enemy', and the other as the defending fleet. No one actually gets hurt, but a lot of valuable lessons are learned.

A convoy of aircraft-carriers, destroyers and frigates on a NATO exercise.

In a recent NATO exercise, a number of 'enemy' ships threatened to invade Norway. The Royal Navy's first task was to transport a large force of Royal Marines, who would help to defend the Norwegian coast. The soldiers were landed by helicopter, along with their equipment, and they quickly took up their positions.

Meanwhile, a close watch was being kept for hostile submarines by *Sea King* helicopters. They searched over a wide area, dropping special sonar devices into the sea to help detect any movements under water. Once an enemy vessel was found, it was 'attacked' with unarmed torpedoes or missiles.

NATO submarines also patrolled the area, preventing further enemy ships from approaching. Minesweepers checked that the main sea routes were free from mines. Vessels bringing supplies to Norway were escorted by frigates. A powerful defence network had been built up in a few days.

An anti-submarine torpedo is dropped from a Sea King *helicopter.*

The Promotion Ladder

Those recruits who join the Navy after leaving school are called Junior Ratings. They immediately become Ordinary Rates at the age of seventeen and a half. Promotion to Able Rate is based both on a person's progress during training and on written tests. After this, promotion depends on age, service record and recommendation.

Ordinary Rate
Age 17½

Able Rate
Age 18½

Leading Rate
Age 22–23

Petty Officer
Age 26–28

Chief Officer
Age 32–35

Fleet Chief Petty Officer
Age 40–45

The Officer badges of the WRNS.

The Officer badges of the Royal Navy.

Most Officers are selected and trained separately from the 'ranks'. They spend two days being examined by a Board of Interviewers before they are accepted. Training takes place at the Royal Naval College at Dartmouth, in Devon. After this the junior Officers, called Midshipmen, join their first ship.

At first, Officers are promoted automatically. By the age of thirty, they may expect to have reached the rank of Lieutenant-Commander and be in charge of a small vessel. However, promotion to Captain and perhaps to Admiral, is gained by only the most outstanding Officers and is earned on merit.

Warships

Aircraft Carriers
The Navy has three aircraft carriers, the latest of which is the *Ark Royal*, completed in 1984. As well as carrying aircraft and helicopters they are equipped with missile systems. In time of war they would act as command ships.

Support Vessels
Other types of vessel are used to carry out a variety of tasks. There are minesweepers, survey boats, tankers for refuelling the fleet and patrol ships which protect fishing areas and oilfields.

Submarines
More than half of the Navy's thirty-four submarines are nuclear-powered. The four *Polaris* submarines carry missiles with nuclear warheads and can stay underwater for long periods. At least one *Polaris* submarine is on patrol at any one time, although its precise location is kept secret.

Assault Ships

HMS *Fearless* (above) and HMS *Intrepid* (right) are ships built to carry a force of soldiers and armoured vehicles. At the stern of each ship is an area that can be flooded to enable a landing craft to be launched. In addition, helicopters can take off from the flight deck.

Destroyers and Frigates

There are more than fifty destroyers and frigates in service (right). Their job is to defend the fleet against attacks from the air, from submarines, or from other surface ships. They are armed with guided missiles, guns and torpedoes, and some also carry helicopters. On average, they have about two hundred and fifty crew members.

Aircraft and Weapons

Aircraft

The *Sea Harrier*, or 'jump jet' (left), has been an enormous success. It needs only a very short runway and can, if necessary, take off and land vertically from a carrier's flight deck. It can be used for defending a ship against air attacks, or for striking at enemy vessels.

However, the number of 'fixed-wing' aircraft used by the Royal Navy has fallen during the 1980s. Helicopters now have a much larger role to play, as they can be carried by both destroyers and frigates. The *Sea King* helicopter (left) is equipped to search out and destroy enemy submarines, and also to give early warning of approaching ships and aircraft.

The lighter *Lynx* helicopter (left) is even more versatile. It can be used to carry torpedoes or missiles to attack enemy ships, or to perform search and rescue missions at sea. It can land safely on a small flight deck, even in the roughest weather.

Weapons

The largest and most powerful of the Navy's weapons is the *Polaris* missile. This carries a nuclear warhead, and can be fired from under the water at a target over 4,000 km (2,500 miles) away.

Surface ships carry a variety of missiles. Some, such as the *Seacat* (above), are designed to destroy aircraft. Others, such as the deadly *Exocet*, are used to attack other ships.

Aircraft, frigates and submarines are all armed with torpedoes. The most advanced of these is the *Stingray*. This can travel deep under the water, and has its own computer to guide it to its target.

The Navy and the World

Since 1945, the Royal Navy has become much smaller. It no longer has the warships or the men with which to 'rule the waves' around the world. Many overseas bases have been closed down, among them Singapore, Malta, Mauritius, Simonstown (in South Africa) and Colombo.

However, the British fleet still has to be prepared to go into action in almost any part of the world. When the Falkland Islands were seized by Argentina in 1982, a 'task force' was immediately formed. It was led by the Navy's three aircraft carriers which, along with other vessels carrying troops and equipment, made the 12,800 km (8,000 mile) journey from Britain in only a few days.

In times of war, the Navy's main job would be to patrol the north-eastern area of the Atlantic, between Greenland and Norway. As part of the NATO forces, British ships would hope to stop enemy warships attacking from the east and threatening the trade routes to Britain and Europe.

Most of the Royal Navy fleet is therefore based in the North Atlantic. Along with the ships of other NATO countries, it keeps a close watch on the movements of the Warsaw Pact forces. British vessels also guard oil and gas platforms in the North Sea.

There are now only two Naval bases left overseas, at Gibraltar and Hong Kong. But small groups of ships are still stationed in the Indian Ocean, the Caribbean and the Antarctic.

An oil rig patrol ship (top left); HMS Endeavour *in the South Atlantic (top right); HMS* Hermes *on route to the Falklands (left); a fisheries protection vessel (right).*

The Future

Like the other British armed forces, the Royal Navy is changing very rapidly. Today, it has far fewer ships and personnel than it had twenty years ago. The numbers are still shrinking. However, the Navy is being equipped with weapons and communications systems that are more powerful than ever before.

The most important change that is planned to occur in the near future will be the arrival of the *Trident* submarine. There will be four of these, each carrying sixteen *Trident* missiles. Each missile will have up to eight nuclear warheads, and a range of 7,400 km (4,600 miles).

The new submarines will replace the *Polaris* submarines. The *Trident* missile will have a much greater range than the *Polaris* missile, so the submarine will be able to operate much further away from the target. The whole project is expected to cost at least £6,000 million.

Other new missiles will also come into use in the late 1980s. The *Sea Eagle* missile can be fired from the *Sea Harrier* and travels faster than the speed of sound. It is guided to its target by its own tiny

The Trident *submarine.*

The Type 23 *frigate, which will carry* Lynx *anti-submarine helicopters.*

computer. The deadly *Sea Wolf*, used for bringing down enemy missiles, is likely to be fitted to more warships.

With so much money being spent on new submarines, few surface ships will be built over the next few years. However a new kind of frigate, the *Type 23*, is now being developed. It will carry special sonar equipment to help track enemy submarines.

Glossary

Command ship The ship in which the leader of an expedition sails and which is used as the headquarters of the operation.

Commando A small fighting force trained for swift raids on areas held by the enemy: also, a member of that force.

Commission A document signed by the Queen and presented to an Officer in the armed forces: it gives him or her certain powers as an Officer.

Destroyer A light, fast warship; nowadays it is usually armed with guided missiles.

Flight deck The upper deck of an aircraft carrier, used as a runway; also, the small deck on a frigate or destroyer used by helicopters.

Frigate A high-speed warship, mostly used to search out and destroy enemy submarines.

Guided missile A rocket which can be controlled after it has been launched.

Ironclad A name for the earliest wooden warships to be armoured with iron plates, and for the first all-metal warships.

Minesweeper A ship specially equipped to seek out and remove dangerous mines.

Nuclear warhead The part of a missile which contains the explosive charge, causing a nuclear explosion.

Pact An agreement.

Radar A way of detecting distant objects using radio waves.

Rating An ordinary seaman.

Sonar A system using sound waves to detect objects underneath the water.

Torpedo An underwater missile fired from a ship or aircraft.

Warsaw Pact A military alliance of Eastern European countries.

Watch The day at sea is divided into six watches of four hours each: bells are rung every half hour – one after half an hour, two after an hour and so on. Midday is always 'eight bells'.

Further Information

If you are interested in finding out more about the Royal Navy, you can get in touch with your local Royal Navy Careers Information Office. The address is in the phone book under 'Naval Establishments'.

Books to Read

Encyclopedia of the Modern Royal Navy by Paul Beaver (Patrick Stephens, 1983)

Nuclear Submarine: The Inside Story by Mike Rossiter (Collins, 1984)

Sailor by Andrew Langley & Chris Fairclough (Franklin Watts, 1986)

The Story of the Navy by Anthony Hobbs (Wayland, 1974)

Picture Acknowledgements

The pictures were supplied by: Camera Press London (Leonard Bourne) 12 (right), 23 (top, right); (Port/News) 22 (top), 27 (bottom left); Central Office of Information 15; Crown Copyright by permission of the Ministry of Defence 20; Michael Holford 6, 7; Crown Copyright 4, 5, 12 (left), 13 (left), 14, 16, 17, 18, 19, 22 (middle and bottom), 23 (top right, bottom), 24 (all), 25, 27 (both top, bottom right) 28, 29; TOPHAM 13 (right). Artwork is by Syd Lewis 8–9, 10–11; Malcolm Walker 21.

Index

British Empire 7

Careers in the Royal Navy
   Careers Office 14
   promotion 20, 21
   special trades 8–11, 15
   tests 14
   training
      Royal Navy 15, 21
      WRNS 15

Engineering 10, 15
Exercises 18

Falklands, the 26

Helicopters
   Lynx 5, 24, 29
   Sea King 19, 24
HMS *Ark Royal* cover
HMS *Bristol* 17
HMS *Dreadnought* 7
HMS *Illustrious* 4
HMS *Intrepid* 23
HMS *Sirius* 5

Missiles
   Exocet 25
   Polaris 25, 28
   Seacat 25
   Sea Eagle 28
   Sea Wolf 28
   Stingray 25
   Trident 28

NATO 4, 5, 18, 19

Officers 21

Press Gangs 7

Ranks 20
Role of the Navy
   abroad 26, 27
   history 5, 6, 7
   in British Empire 7
   in defence 4, 5
   in First World War 7
   in Second World War 7
   in the future 28, 29
   organization 8–11
   size 4
   with NATO 4, 5, 18, 19, 26
Royal Marines
   commando units 12, 13
   on exercise 19
   role 12
   relationship to Navy 12
   Special Boat Service 13
   training 13
Royal Navy
   Communications Group 9
   engineering 10
   Fleet Air Arm 9
   medical 11
   Seamen Group 8
   Supply Branch 10

Sea Harrier 24, 28
Seaman
   daily duties 16, 17
   front line 8, 9
   history 6, 7
   living conditions 7, 17
   ranks 20
   support branches 10, 11
Ships 4, 16, 17, 18, 19
   aircraft-carriers 4, 18, 22
   assault ships 23
   destroyers and frigates 19, 23
   history of 6, 7
   ironclads 7
   patrol 27
   support 22
   type 23, 29
Submarines 22
   Polaris 22, 28
   Trident 28

Torpedoes 19
Trafalgar, battle of 6, 7

Watches 16
WRNS 11, 15, 20